Exploring the World of Animals

TRY THIS!

by Penny Raife Durant
Illustrated by Nancy Woodman

D1532905

A *Try This* Book
Franklin Watts
New York ❖ Chicago ❖ London ❖ Toronto ❖ Sydney

**To my brother, Michael,
and his wife Nancy, with love.**

Cover illustration copyright © Nancy Woodman

Photographs copyright ©:
Comstock, Inc.: pp. 6 (Russ Kinne), 10 (George Lepp), 11 (Stuart Cohen), 27 (Denver Bryan), 44 (Georg Gerster); Visuals Unlimited, Inc.: pp. 9 (Barbara Gerlach), 14 (Cabisco), 21, 28 (both John D. Cunningham), 23, 32 (both Richard C. Walters), 29 (Joe McDonald), 34 (William J. Weber), 35 (John Gerlach); U.S. Fish and Wildlife Service: pp. 18, 19; Tom Stack and Associates: p. 40 (David M. Dennis).

Library of Congress Cataloging-in-Publication Data Durant, Penny Raife.

Exploring the world of animals / by Penny Raife Durant;
illustrations by Nancy Woodman.
p. cm. — (Try this !)
Includes index.
ISBN 0-531-20128-7 (lib. bdg.).— ISBN 0-531-15744-X (pbk.)
1. Animals—Juvenile literature. 2. Zoology—Juvenile literature.
3. Animals—Experiments—Juvenile literature. 4. Zoology—
Experiments—Juvenile literature. [1. Animals. 2. Zoology. 3. Animals—Experiments.
4. Experiments.] I. Woodman, Nancy ill. II. Title. III. Series: Try this series.
QL49.D86 1995
591—dc20   94-49664
                                                                    CIP   AC

Exploring the World of Animals

CONTENTS

Gorillas and humans are alike in many ways. That is why scientists call them both primates.

THE WORLD OF ANIMALS

Did you know that you are an animal? You are part of the Animal Kingdom. An earthworm is an animal, too. But you are very different from an earthworm. There are many differences among animals, but there are things that are the same for all animals. We all have certain basic needs, like food and water. How we get them can be very different.

Scientists have divided all life into groups. All animals are part of the Animal Kingdom. All plants are part of the Plant Kingdom. The kingdoms are divided into smaller groups. The members of each group are alike in some way.

Mammals are one group of animals. Within the group of mammals is the group of primates. Humans and apes are primates. Every animal that we know is a member of some group. Whenever new animals are found, scientists determine the group to which the animal belongs. They classify it.

Scientists sometimes classify animals according to

where they live. Rain forest communities differ from desert communities. These communities are called *biomes*. (You can look up the pronunciation and meaning of any word in *italics* in the glossary in the back of the book.) Each biome promotes the growth of certain kinds of plants and animals.

This book will take you on a journey into the world of animals. You'll discover some of the things that make us animals. You'll see the relationship between animals and people. You'll get a chance to try many activities. Scientists who work with animals are called *zoologists*. Be a zoologist, and try these activities!

WHAT ANIMALS NEED

Every living thing has certain basic needs. All animals need food, clean air, shelter, water, and personal space.

Food

What do animals eat? Animals have different diets. Some eat only meat. They are called *carnivores*. Some eat only plants. They are *herbivores*. *Insectivores* eat only insects. Animals that eat both plants and meat are called *omnivores*. Can you think of animals that fit each category?

One clue to what an animal eats is its teeth. An animal's teeth are adapted to its diet.

Like all animals, these baby robins need food to live.

Look at the teeth in your pet's mouth. Look at photographs and drawings of the teeth of other animals.

Which animals have sharp, pointed teeth? Sharp teeth are needed for biting and tearing flesh. Which ani-

A mountain lion has sharp teeth that are good for eating meat.

A horse has wide teeth that are good for grinding grass.

mals have wide, flat teeth? Flat teeth are good for grinding plant food. Which kind of teeth would a horse have? A cow? A lion? Why?

Look into a mirror at your own teeth. Think about what you eat. Which teeth do you use to tear or bite? Which teeth grind your food? Bite into an apple, then chew it. Which teeth did you use to bite it? Which to chew?

Birds do not have teeth. Their food is ground up in an organ called a *gizzard*. Chickens are a kind of bird, and they have gizzards. When they pick up pieces of seed off the ground to eat, they also get little pieces of rocks. The rocks help grind the food in their gizzards.

Birds have differently shaped bills and beaks. The shape can tell us what the bird eats.

Look at the different bird beaks and bills on this page. Which type of beak would be best for tearing flesh?

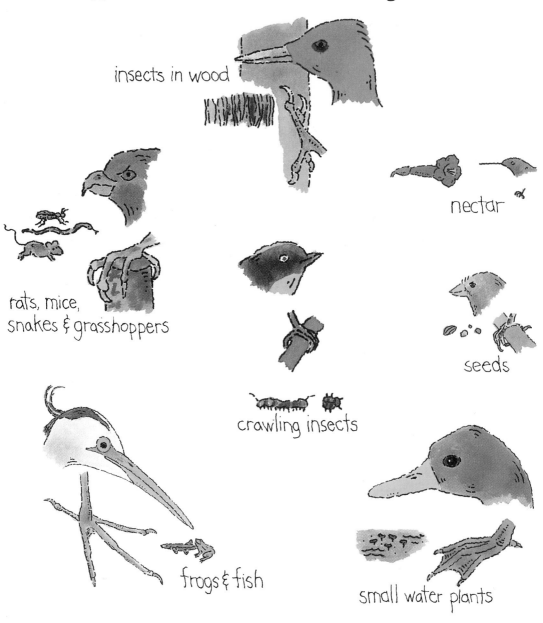

insects in wood

nectar

rats, mice, snakes & grasshoppers

seeds

crawling insects

frogs & fish

small water plants

Which would be good for cracking seeds? Which bill could scoop plants from the water? Which would be good for searching out insects and worms? To see if you are right, look in each drawing for the food the bird eats.

Can you think of birds that have each type of bill? Use a field guide to birds from your library to check.

A bird's feet can also tell you what the bird eats. A heron has feet that are adapted for wading in shallow water. It spears and eats small fish in the water. A grosbeak has feet for perching on trees or bushes, where it finds berries to eat.

Turkeys and roadrunners have feet for running after insects and small animals. A hawk or other bird of prey has talons for grasping small animals. A duck could never grasp a mouse in its webbed feet and carry it off. The duck's webbed feet help it move through the water to find water plants to eat.

Air

Animals need clean air to breathe. What happens when the air is polluted? Humans can get lung cancer from dirty air. Fumes can kill birds. Miners used to carry a bird in a cage with them into their tunnels. If the air became poisoned, the bird would die. Then the miners knew they had to get out fast.

Air pollution can also cause rain to be poisoned. Then the water supply for plants and animals is poisoned. Fish in the lakes and ponds die. Trees die.

Grass dies. The homes and food for animals die, so they can't live, either.

Why do earthworms come up from underground after a rain?

How do we know animals need air? Some animals have nostrils we can see. It is easy to watch your dog breathe. But what about an earthworm? Does it need air, too?

Try this:

Fill a clear glass with gravel. Slowly add enough water to cover the gravel. What happens? Do you see bubbles rise from between the rocks? The water forces all the air out of the spaces between the gravel.

Now take a container of earthworms and soil. If you don't have earthworms in your yard, you can get a container of earthworms in soil from a sporting-goods store. Add water. If you add too much, what do the earthworms do?

After a rain, earthworms come up out of the ground. They are searching for air. Just as water did in the gravel, rain fills the spaces in the ground with water. When the spaces no longer hold air, the earthworm has to come to the surface for air. Did your earthworm come out of the soil?

What could you do for earthworms that lie on a sidewalk after a rain? If they stay there too long, they will dry out and die. Where is the best place to move them?

Water

Clean water is important to animals. You drink clean water from your kitchen. You change your dog's or cat's water every day. What about other animals? Where do they get their water? Some animals get enough water in the food they eat. Some get water that beads up on plants after a rain. Many drink from streams and ponds.

Some animals, like camels, can go for long periods of time without water. People can't. We need to drink plenty of clean water every day.

Shelter

Animals need shelter. Some squirrels live in trees. Some burrow in the ground. Bears must find shelter for the long winter months when they sleep. You live in a heated house or apartment. How can you tell if wildlife is living near you? Can you find the shelters of animals?

Try this:

Try this only if you live outside a city. Gather some food that appeals to animals. This might include seeds, dog or cat food, or pieces of your food. Leave the food outside on a flat cookie sheet. Sprinkle flour around the food. Leave it overnight. Check the next morning for tracks. Did something visit your food? Can you tell what animals were there? What was eaten? If you don't have any visitors, try again with a different type of food.

Take a walk around your yard or neighborhood. Look for animals. Most wildlife will hide from you. How can you tell if it has been there? Look for evidence! A spider web tells you a spider lives there even if you don't see a spider.

Dead insects, feathers, nests, tracks, and droppings all tell you that animal life has been there. You can also look for the homes of animals. Many birds make nests in

Some racoons live in the holes of trees.

🐾 🐾 🐾 🐾 🐾 🐾 🐾 🐾

trees, and raccoons and porcupines live in holes in trees
or in hollow logs. Ants make hills, and ant lions make
pits in soft sand. Do you find any evidence of wildlife?

Try this: 🐾 🐾 🐾 🐾 🐾 🐾

Do this one with an adult. Wash a large, empty
coffee can. Carefully remove the bottom using
a can opener. Stretch a piece of clear plastic
wrap over one end. Hold it tightly
in place with a rubber band.
If you have a large glass
jar, you can use it
instead of the can.

Stand quietly in the shallow part of a pond. Put the can into the water with the plastic-wrapped end first. Or put the bottom of the jar in first. Don't let water get into the can or jar. Look through the plastic wrap window or jar. Try looking under a rock or in the plants at the water's edge. Do you find any animal life in the pond?

Personal Space

Animals need personal space. Wild animals shy away when we walk near them. They have their own territory. What happens then when new houses are built near a forest or field? The more people there are, the less room there is for wildlife. People take land for

Coyotes have adapted well to people moving into their territory. They prey on small animals such as sheep kept by ranchers.

homes and businesses. They also take over land for growing crops and grazing herds. This changes the environment for wildlife.

Some animals adapt to the changes. One animal that has adapted well to changes brought by people is the coyote. Coyotes *prey* on small livestock kept by ranchers. Pigeons have learned to get food in cities. Other animals do not adapt and move deeper into forests and uninhabited places. Still others die out when their natural homes are lost.

Try this:

Take a trip to the zoo. Visit several animals to look at where they live—their *habitat*. Do you think the zoo habitat is like their natural habitat? In the wild, giraffes eat leaves from trees. How do they eat at the zoo? What about carnivores, such as the big cats? How are the habitats made to look like the animal's natural world? What improvements would you suggest?

ANIMALS AND ADAPTATIONS

You can observe wildlife as a zoologist does. You may discover that animals have interesting features that help them survive in their world. You can observe wildlife at the zoo or you can do it in your own neighborhood. Even in big cities there are birds.

Try this: 🐾 🐾

Take a notebook and a pen or pencil. Go outside and watch for birds. Write down the names of the birds if you know them. Write down other

A giraffe's long neck helps it eat leaves high on trees.

important information as well. What time is it? What color are the birds? What markings do they have? What is the shape of their tails? Beaks? Wings?

Where did you see them? Was it in a tree? On a park bench? Walking on the ground? How did they fly? Did they glide? Did they sing? What did it sound like? Take lots of notes. What time is it when you first hear birds singing in the morning? Where do birds go at night?

These notes are called *field notes*. You can go out again at another time and take more field notes. The next time, you will probably notice something different.

It is a good idea to date your notes. Make a comment about the weather. Is it sunny or cloudy? Raining? What season is it? Go to the same spot in *every* season. Do you see the same kind of birds? If the same birds are there, do they behave the same in different seasons? Are there new, smaller ones?

You can also take field notes on animals at the zoo. Can you tell the males from the females? Are there any young ones? When you make field notes, it is important to be patient. Don't hurry, or you might miss something important.

In your yard, you might find sow bugs, or "roly-poly" bugs. Look under a small planter or a piece of decaying wood. If you don't see any, leave a corncob on the ground overnight. Any sow bugs in the yard should gather under the corncob.

You may find a sow bug on the ground underneath a decaying piece of wood.

Examine a sow bug with a magnifying glass. What color is it? How many legs does it have? Can you find its mouth? What happens when you touch it? How large is the largest one? How small is the smallest? Keep notes in your notebook. What seems to be the sow bug's favorite place in your yard? When you are finished with the bug, put it back in its favorite place.

An insect that is interesting to observe is the grasshopper. But to observe grasshoppers and keep them safe, you'll first have to get a home for them. You can either buy a bug house or make your own.

Try this:

The simplest bug house is a canning jar. It should be large enough to hold your insect plus a twig and several leaves. To allow air to enter the jar, cut a square of cloth to cover the mouth of the jar. Use a fabric like cheesecloth that lets air through. Screw the ring of the lid onto the canning jar over the cloth to keep it in place.

You can also make a bug house from two plastic margarine tubs, window screen, and plaster of paris. Cut a nine-inch square of window screen. Form a tube by stapling two opposite sides of the screen together. Stir a little water into a half cup of plaster of paris in one of the margarine tubs. The mixture should be a little thicker than pancake batter. Stand the screen tube in the plaster and let it dry. Use the second margarine tub as a cap to keep the insect inside the screen until you release it outdoors.

Then catch a grasshopper. You will find one in midsummer on leaves in your yard or park. If you can't catch one or if it is too cold for grasshoppers, you can buy crickets at a pet store. Make sure your insect gets plenty of air and fresh green leaves in its bug house.

Take a good look at its head, legs, wings, and body. Can you see the three sections of its body? It has a head, an *abdomen,* and a *thorax* between the abdomen and the head. Can you tell anything about its mouth? What does a grasshopper eat? Does it make a noise? Does it have antennae?

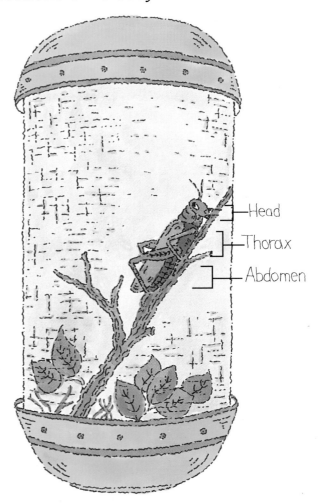

—Head

—Thorax

—Abdomen

What color is the grasshopper? How would its colors help protect it? Keep notes in your notebook. Then let the grasshopper go outside. How does it move? Can you measure how far it moves?

What's on the Outside

Was the grasshopper's body covered with fur? Was its body hard? Have you ever accidentally stepped on a cricket or grasshopper? Did you hear a cracking sound? An insect has no bones. Its outer, hard covering is called an *exoskeleton*. The exoskeleton protects the soft inside of the insect.

Other animals have different coverings. An earthworm has a soft, pliable covering that moves easily. Many animals have furry coverings. A tortoise has a shell. So do many other sea creatures. Most fish are covered with scales. You have skin, but no fur. Can you guess why certain animals have the coverings they do?

Body coverings serve the unique needs of each type of animal. The grasshopper is born in the spring, lays eggs in the fall, and then dies before winter comes. It does not need a furry coat to stay warm as do the bear, deer, and sheep. But some animals live through the winter without fur. What does a turtle, a frog, or a fish do in winter?

Each difference in body covering is called an *adaptation*. An adaptation is a body part that developed, or evolved, over many years. The animal teeth and bird beaks we talked about earlier are adaptations. Adaptations make it easier for an animal to live in its environment. Animals that do not adapt to their environment die out.

Animal bodies have adapted to help animals move in certain ways. Your body was made to walk on just two feet. This gives you the freedom to use your hands for other things. The cheetah's hips and legs give it speed for short distances. Because of this, the cheetah is the fastest land animal. The shape of a swift's body makes it the fastest bird.

A cheetah is built for speed, with narrow hips and large, powerful legs.

Getting Food

All animals need food to eat. Some get their food by grazing, or eating plants. Some, like the frog, snatch food as it goes by. The spider must build a web and wait for something to get caught in it.

Instead of teeth, blue whales have baleen in their mouths. Baleen is a comb of tiny bones that trap small

The broomlike baleen in this whale's mouth helps it trap shrimp and plankton.

shrimp and plankton. The huge whale swims through the water with its mouth open. It takes in large quantities of water as it goes. Then, with its enormous tongue, it pushes the water out through the baleen. Whatever is caught inside gets eaten when the whale swallows.

Some animals have to hunt for food. They are called *predators.*

Protection

If you are an animal that is hunted, what can you do to protect yourself? A rabbit can run very fast, faster than a fox that's chasing it. Rabbits also have large ears so they can hear foxes from a great distance. Foxes learn to be very quiet when they hunt rabbits.

Some animals have body structures that protect them. How would a spiny animal like a porcupine or spiny fish keep safe? Think about special adaptations such as the skunk's odor and the octopus's ink. The shell of a turtle protects it from many animals, but not from people. Bee and wasp stingers keep people and other animals away from their hives and nests.

Some animals' coloring will protect them. A fawn, or baby deer, is born with spots. The spots help hide it in the leaves and bushes. A chameleon changes color to blend with the colors surrounding it. A katydid is an insect that looks like a leaf. All these are types of *camouflage*.

Look at the photograph below. Can you find the animal hidden in it?

Can you find the chameleon?

29

Scatter small beads of various colors on a piece of colored paper. Then have a friend time you while you pick them up. How many beads can you pick up, one at a time, in thirty seconds? Count how many of each color

you picked up. Do this again with the same beads. Let your friend do the picking up, while you do the timing.

Then change the color of the paper under the beads and try again. Compare your findings. Did you pick up any beads that were the same color as the paper? Which beads were easiest to see and pick up? An animal's color can help it blend in as the beads did with the paper.

Another type of protection is called *mimicry*. That is when an animal looks like another animal. There is a type of fly that looks a lot like a bumblebee. Any animal that has tangled with a bumblebee will leave the fly alone. Some fish have large spots near their back ends. These spots look like eyes and make the fish look much larger than they are. Mimicry sometimes fools predators.

Another interesting adaptation is an animal's eyes.

Try this:

Use a magnifying glass to look at a picture from a newspaper. Can you see all the dots that make up the photo? This is a lot like what an insect's eyes see. Everything is broken into pieces. Another way you can see this is to look through a multifaceted lens. You may be able to buy one in a museum gift shop. Seeing things in pieces helps insects detect motion quickly. With this kind of vision, they are likely to escape predators.

Look at the large, round mirror in the corner of a store. Do you see the straight aisles bend and curve? The mirror lets the clerk see more of the store. Fish have round eyes like this mirror so they can see more of what's around them.

Whose eyes see better to the sides? One answer is a horse. Can you think of any others? These animals can see predators chasing them from behind more easily than we can.

The tiny segments of this horsefly's eyes help it detect predators quickly.

When you use both your eyes, you have three-dimensional eyesight. Some animals don't need three-dimensional eyesight. They are better off being able to look in two directions at once. One such animal is the lizard. Its eyes don't move together, so it can look for predators or prey in two directions at the same time.

SEASONS

Seasons and temperature affect animals. They react to heat and cold. Have you visited the zoo in two different seasons? Did you notice any changes in behavior?

Try this:

Take an *inventory* of animals in your neighborhood or park. An inventory is a list of all the animals you see. Write down what they are doing. Revisit the same area in a few months. What changes do you observe? If you don't live near a park or yard, you can still observe animals. You can observe people! What changes do you see in people in different seasons?

Some animals leave an area during the cold months. Many birds leave for warmer climates in the fall. We call this *migration*. Robins and snow geese migrate. Whales migrate great distances in the ocean.

Other animals do not move as far as birds or whales. Deer move from summer to winter grazing areas that

Every spring, these cranes migrate north together.

are close to each other. What would happen if someone built a road that divided the two grazing areas?

Some animals sleep for most of the winter. We call this *hibernation*. Bears and squirrels hibernate. The dormouse sleeps for five or six months!

Some animals sleep in the heat and dryness of summer. We call this *estivation*. Some frogs, toads, and snails estivate by burrowing into mud. The mud dries during the heat and then softens when the rains come again. That allows the animals to come out of the mud.

What happens to fish in winter?

*Sleeping buried in the mud in summer
keeps some toads from drying out.*

Try this:

Get a goldfish and keep it in a fishbowl. Take notes on how the fish moves. How fast does it swim? Put ice cubes in a bowl just larger than the fishbowl. Place the fishbowl in the bowl with ice. Never put the fish directly into much colder or hotter water than the water in which they live. It could kill them. The temperature must change gradually.

Leave the fishbowl in the ice for fifteen minutes. Take notes on the fish again. What changes do you notice? Remove the fishbowl from the ice.

Animals react to heat and cold. Some animals are cold-blooded. This means that their bodies are the same temperature as the air and land around them. Lizards and snakes are cold-blooded. The bodies of warm-blooded animals, including people and other mammals, are at higher temperatures.

Some animals have special adaptations to help them cope with temperature changes. Does your dog's coat get thicker or thinner in the fall? What happens in the spring? Take a piece of masking tape and run it lightly over your dog's fur. Did a lot of hair stick to the tape? Is the dog shedding? This happens with many animals that have fur.

Some animals need to cool off because they live in hot places. How does your dog cool off in summer? A dog doesn't sweat as you do. When you sweat, your body cools off. When a dog breathes heavily with its tongue out, we say it is panting. Panting helps cool a dog. How?

Take a mirror and hold it close to your face. Open your mouth wide and pant. What happens?

Ask an adult to give you some rubbing alcohol and a cotton ball. Put a little of the alcohol on the cotton ball and swab it on your arm. As the alcohol evaporates away, does your skin feel cooler? Try it again on your other arm and blow on it this time to speed up the evaporation.

When you sweat, water evaporates. When the dog breathes over its tongue, water on the tongue evaporates. Evaporating water cools the dog just as evaporating sweat cools you.

Elephants don't pant or sweat. They wave their ears. Why?

How does a polar bear keep warm in the Arctic? For one thing, a polar bear stores fat under its coat. The fat insulates the polar bear.

Fill a glass with ice cubes and water. Add an air temperature thermometer to the glass and leave it for a minute. Record the temperature. Take the thermometer out and let it rise to room temperature again. Then take some butter or margarine and cover the bulb end of the thermometer. Record the temperature of the ice water again.

Now take the thermometer out and let it rise to room temperature. Add more butter or margarine to the end of the thermometer until it is about one-half inch (about a centimeter) thick. Take the temperature again. Does the butter make a difference?

Life Cycles

Other things happen according to the seasons as well. In the spring, take a ride in the country. Do you see lots of new calves and foals? Babies of many mammals and other animals are born in the spring. Why is spring a good time for animals to be born?

Do this early in the spring. Find an *egg case* on a twig. An egg case holds an insect's eggs. Bring the twig inside and put it into a bug house. Watch the egg case and take notes. Be sure to include fresh green leaves in your jar or bug house. After the eggs hatch, watch the new insects for only a day or two before letting them go outside.

Have you ever opened your oatmeal or cracker box and found weevils or tiny worms in it? These are probably mealworms. They may make you want to throw away the food, but don't. You can use it for observing insects.

Try this: 🐾 🐾 🐾 🐾 🐾 🐾

Put some oatmeal on a plate and sort through it with a pencil. If you can find them, take out several live weevils or worms. The worms are *larva* of weevils. Save a little oatmeal for the weevils and worms to eat. Look for opened larva casings. They look striped and are a little smaller than the worms. Use a magnifying glass. Can you find any eggs?

Keep the weevils and mealworms in a container with something to eat. They will eat crackers, oatmeal or other cereals, or flour. After several days you should see each worm turn into a *pupa*. Later, the adult weevils emerge. Did you find all four stages of the weevil in your oatmeal?

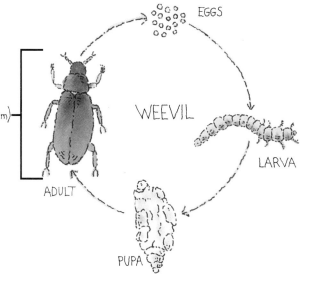

EGGS

WEEVIL

LARVA

¼" (6mm)

ADULT

PUPA

🐾

39

It's possible you won't find mealworms or weevils. If you don't, you can order a butterfly cocoon and a house for hatching butterflies instead. It's important to read the directions carefully and follow them well. And don't forget to let your butterfly go when it's time; you wouldn't want it to die.

What else comes from eggs? Most animals come from eggs. Birds, frogs, and reptiles lay eggs. Eggs grow inside the bodies of people and other mammals. What would happen if the eggs that birds and reptiles lay did not have shells?

The yolk of an egg is a single cell. Open a raw egg. Can you find the white dot in the yolk? That is the *nucleus* of the cell.

Try this: 🐾 🐾 🐾 🐾 🐾 🐾

See if you can find out which animal lays the largest egg. Which bird lays the smallest? Can you find out if a turtle's eggs are larger or smaller than a robin's? Make a chart of ten eggs of different sizes, from the largest to smallest.

Which egg came from an ostrich? A chicken? A hummingbird?

Why are eggs shaped the way they are? Why aren't they round like a ball? Gently roll an egg and a small ball on a table. Which one is likely to fall out of a nest?

How can you tell the age of an animal, such as a fish?

Try this: 🐾   🐾   🐾   🐾   🐾   🐾

The next time your family catches a fish or buys a whole fish, such as a trout, ask for a few of the fish's scales. Let them dry on a paper towel. Use a magnifying glass to look at the scales. Count the wide bands you see. Each year a fish lives, it grows a new band. How old was the fish you bought?

WHAT WE CAN DO

We have seen that all animals eat food. What an animal eats determines its place on the food chain. Look at the illustration of a food chain below. The arrows run from a type of food to the animals that eat it. A mouse eats seeds and other plant life. The mouse is what is called a primary consumer. An owl eats mice so it is a secondary consumer. It is higher on the food chain than a mouse.

Animals high on the food chain take more of the world's resources than those

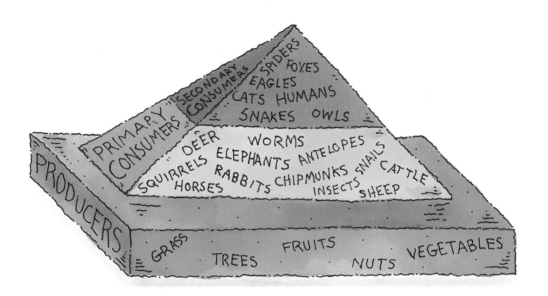

below them. Plants and trees are at the bottom of the food chain. They are called producers because they don't eat other living things. They only produce food for other living things.

People are at the top of the chain. We eat a great deal of food. We could save resources if we ate less meat and more food that is lower on the food chain. Then there might be more food for the hungry people of the world.

Another way to look at the food chain is as a pyramid. It takes many more animals at the bottom of the pyramid to support a few animals at the top.

Try this:

Make a list of the food you eat for one day. Then go over the list. Place each item of food you ate on the food chain or pyramid. Look at your list. Could you eat more food lower on the food chain and still eat a balanced diet?

Endangered Animals

Some animals are dying out. New ones are not being born as fast as the older ones are dying. There are many reasons for this. Some of them have to do with people and what we do to change the environment. When forests are cut down, not only trees are lost. Those trees were homes to animals. As the forests shrink, the animals have little room to live and feed. Fewer animals can live there.

Oil spilled by ships can get in birds' feathers and prevent them from flying.

Humans can cause other problems for animals. Oil spills and acid rain are dangerous for wildlife. Oil spills cover the eggs of seabirds with a black sticky tar. But they do not just damage eggs. Water fowl, or birds that live near water, have special feathers to keep them dry. Without clean, dry feathers, birds cannot fly.

Examine a feather with a magnifying glass. Leave another feather in a bowl of cooking oil for a few minutes. Examine it. How does the oil affect the feather? Run your fingers over both feathers. Separate the barbs. Look at both feathers again. Run your fingers over the barbs to smooth the feather. What happens?

While it seems some people do not care what happens to wildlife, many people care a lot. Some people think endangered species should be bred in zoos. Others think it is best to leave them in the wild. Others try to pass laws that will protect the habitats, or homes, of the animals.

You've seen many different animals and how they satisfy their basic needs. You've observed animals and their habitats. Did you find out which animals have the greatest impact on the others? You're right if you guessed humans. We have the capability to do wonderful and terrible things. Everything we do, from what we choose to eat to what we do to the air, affects other animals. Let's choose to do wonderful things.

GLOSSARY

abdomen (AB-doh-men)—the part of a body containing digestive organs

adaptation (ad-ap-TAY-shun)—a physical feature that evolved to help an animal or group survive in its environment

baleen (buh-LEEN)—whalebone in the mouths of certain whales, used to strain food from seawater

biome (BY-ome)—a region of the earth with specific climate, plants, and animals

camouflage (KAM-o-flahj)—to hide by blending in with the surroundings

carnivore (KAR-nuh-vore)—an animal that feeds on other animals

cold-blooded animal—an animal whose blood temperature ranges from freezing upward, depending on the outside temperature

estivation (es-tuh-VAY-shun)—passing the summer in sleep

exoskeleton (ek-soh-SKEL-uh-tun)—a hard protective covering

field notes—notes scientists take when they are making observations outside, in the field

gizzard (GIZ-erd)—an organ in birds that grinds food

habitat (HAB-uh-tat)—the place where an animal lives

herbivore (ER-buh-vore)—an animal that feeds on plants

hibernation (hie-ber-NAY-shun)—a state of constant sleep experienced by some animals during the winter

insectivore (in-SEK-tih-vore)—an animal that feeds on insects

inventory (IN-ven-tore-ee)—a list of everything in a store, building, or other area.

larva (LAR-va)—the wormlike stage of an insect's life after it has hatched from an egg

migration (my-GRAY-shun)—the seasonal movement of birds and other animals from one region to another

mimicry (MIM-uh-kree)—the close resemblance of one animal to another, for protection

nucleus (NOO-klee-us)—the central part of a cell; the nucleus directs cell activity

predator (PRED-uh-tore)—an animal that preys on other animals

prey (PRAY)—to hunt another animal, or: an animal that is hunted by another animal.

pupa (PYOO-puh)—the stage of an insect's life before it becomes an adult

thorax (THORE-aks)—the part of an insect's body between the head and abdomen

warm-blooded animal—an animal whose blood temperature remains constant and is not influenced by outside temperature

zoologist (zoh-ALL-uh-jist)—a scientist who works with animals

INDEX

Numbers in *italics* indicate illustrations.